This book belongs to

....

*To all the cetacean conservationists of the world.
Thank you for helping to protect these wonderful creatures. – K.P.*

*For all those young explorers who are curious
about the world beneath the waves... – B.H.*

Published in 2025 by Welbeck Children's Books
An imprint of Hachette Children's Group,
Part of Hodder & Stoughton Limited
Carmelite House, 50 Victoria Embankment
London EC4Y 0DZ

An Hachette UK Company
www.hachette.co.uk
www.hachettechildrens.co.uk

Text © 2025 Kate Peridot
Illustration © 2025 Becca Hall

Kate Peridot and Becca Hall have asserted their moral rights
to be identified as the author and illustrator of this Work in
accordance with the Copyright Designs and Patents Act 1988.

All rights reserved. No part of this publication may be reproduced,
stored in a retrieval system, or transmitted in any form or by any means,
electronically, mechanical, photocopying, recording, or otherwise, without
the prior permission of the copyright owners and the publishers.

A CIP catalogue record for this book is available from the British Library.

HB ISBN: 978-1-80453-705-3
E-Book: 978-1-80453-799-2

Printed in China

1 3 5 7 9 10 8 6 4 2

The website addresses (URLs) included in this book were valid at the time of going to press. However,
it is possible that contents or addresses may have changed since the publication of this book.
No responsibility for any such changes can be accepted by either the author or the publisher.

Meet the WHALES

KATE PERIDOT • BECCA HALL

WELBECK
CHILDREN'S BOOKS

You come from a family of sailors, ocean explorers, and underwater filmmakers.

Now you want to head out onto the water and join Captain Grandma on an expedition to film the world's biggest and smartest creatures, the whales.

To prove you're ready, you've been practicing all the skills needed for a long sea voyage.

Finding your sea legs.

Safety at sea.

Swimming and snorkeling.

Filming sea creatures.

Reading about cetaceans.

Congratulations. You're on the team!

Arctic Pack Ice Sled
(Narwhal)

Canadian Canoe
(Orca)

Atlantic Yacht
(Bottlenose Dolphin)

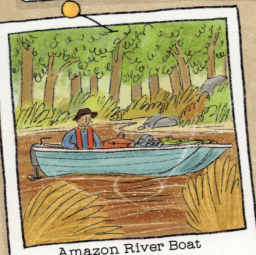

Amazon River Boat
(Amazon River Dolphin)

Antarctic Research Ship
(Blue Whale)

Indian Ocean Submarine
(Sperm Whale)

Together you decide on the eight whales you're going to see—and plan how to reach them!

Australian Rigid Hulled
Inflatable Boat (Humpback Whale)

South China Sea Snorkeling
(Indo-Pacific Finless Porpoise)

The first boat casts off from the dock at dawn and it's going to be a while until your feet are back on dry land, so double-check you have everything on your ocean explorer kit list.

IT'S TIME TO MEET THE WHALES.

Snorkel, mask, and fins

Life jacket

Safety harness and tether

Camera, underwater case, and pole

Hydrophone & earphones (to listen for whale song)

Binoculars

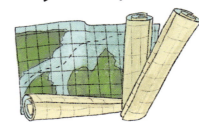
Sea charts

Seasickness medicine

Whale watching guide

I want to make my own movie about one of the whales, but I don't know which one to choose.

Crunch! Our ship is stuck in the Arctic sea ice. We climb down the ladder and ride on a dogsled over the bumpy ground. Our guide takes us to an open fissure of narrow sea. A long pointy tusk rises out of the water as a male and his family surface. They snort and jostle for space, the breath from their blowholes clouding in the freezing air.

Meet the NARWHAL.

🐟 PREY:

Polar cod

Shrimp

Greenland halibut

Gonatus squid

King crab

🐟 TYPE:
Toothed whale. All toothed whales have teeth. The group includes dolphins and porpoises.

🐟 HOW TO SPOT A NARWHAL:

Only males have a single long tusk.

No dorsal fin and short tail flukes.

Adults have black and white spotted skin and a white underbelly.

A rounded head and sausage-shaped body.

Calves are born blue/gray.

🐟 RANGE: The Arctic Circle.

Would you like to film this **whale**?

No, his tusk is too pointy.

We paddle along the rocky shore towards shallow water where whales enjoy rubbing their tummies on smooth stones. Tall dorsal fins rise out of the water and with a splash of their tails, the family take it in turns to dive down. Then a mother and calf turn toward us and speed-swim right under our canoes, curious to see who we are.

Meet the ORCA.

The orca is also called a killer whale because she is an expert hunter.

The most experienced female leads a family pod of up to 40 whales.

Her pod has lots of smart hunting tricks. They herd fish into shoals, so they are easier to catch, and they make waves with their tails to bump prey (a penguin or sea lion) off an ice floe.

Her language of clicks, whistles, squeals, squeaks, and screams are unique to her family.

She has about 45 sharp interlocking teeth for catching all kinds of prey.

- **TYPE:** Toothed whale and the largest member of the dolphin family.

- **HOW TO SPOT AN ORCA:**

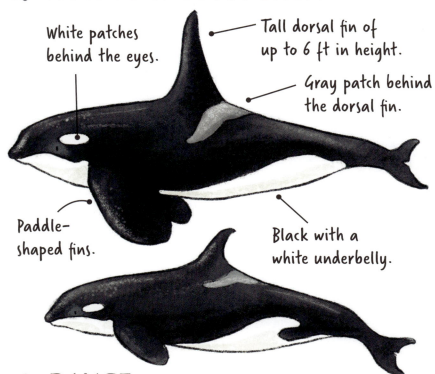

White patches behind the eyes.
Tall dorsal fin of up to 6 ft in height.
Gray patch behind the dorsal fin.
Paddle-shaped fins.
Black with a white underbelly.

- **RANGE:** They live in every ocean in the world but prefer cooler waters. Some pods stay in the same region all year, other pods migrate hundreds of miles to find food.

Would you like to film these **whales**?

No, they have too many sharp teeth!

- **PREY:** Each pod has a preferred food depending on where they live.

Salmon
Squid
Ray
Cormorant
Young great white shark
Octopus
King penguin
Sea lion

The riverboat glides around the bend and cuts the engine. You put an underwater camera on the end of a pole over the side of the boat. A smiling pink face comes over to inspect this strange new object, and then he grabs the camera in his mouth and swims off with it!

Meet the AMAZON RIVER DOLPHIN.

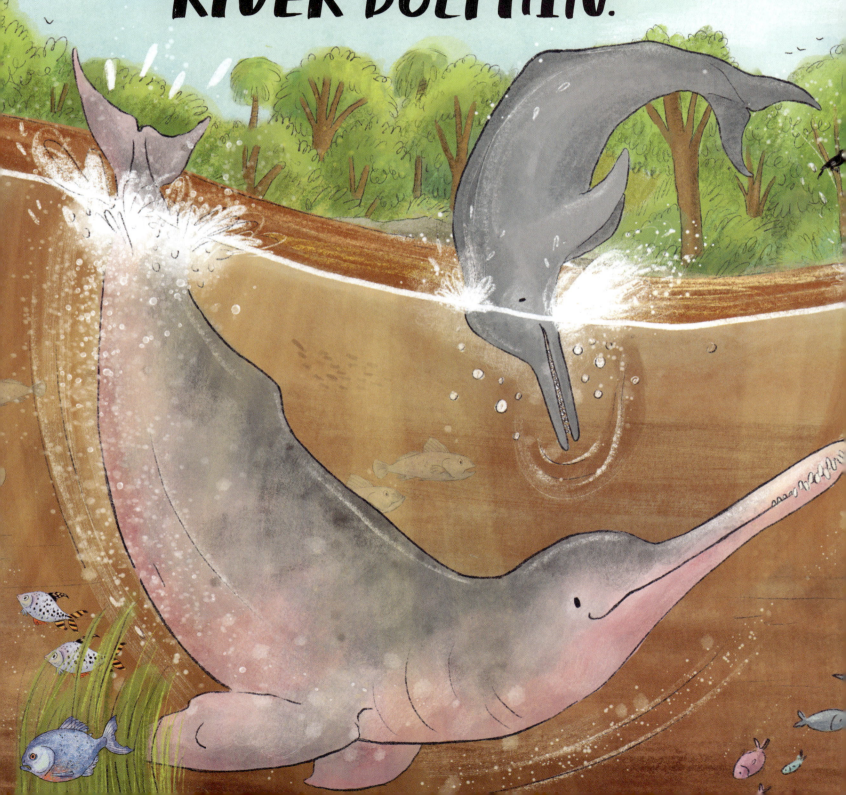

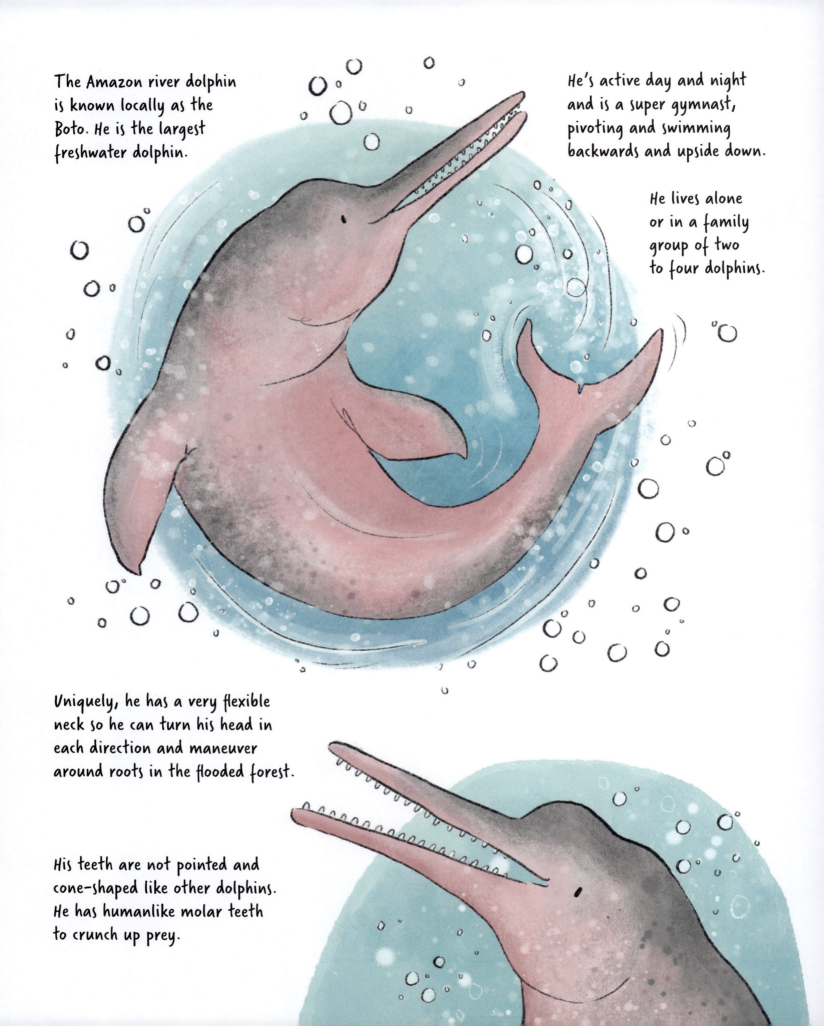

The Amazon river dolphin is known locally as the Boto. He is the largest freshwater dolphin.

He's active day and night and is a super gymnast, pivoting and swimming backwards and upside down.

He lives alone or in a family group of two to four dolphins.

Uniquely, he has a very flexible neck so he can turn his head in each direction and maneuver around roots in the flooded forest.

His teeth are not pointed and cone-shaped like other dolphins. He has humanlike molar teeth to crunch up prey.

PREY:

- Characin
- Catfish
- Tetra
- Amazon freshwater mollusc
- Piranha
- Aquatic frog
- Croaker
- Shrimp
- Amazon freshwater crab

HOW TO SPOT AN AMAZON RIVER DOLPHIN:

An enlarged rounded forehead and chubby cheeks.

Long skinny snout with whiskers for rooting through river mud.

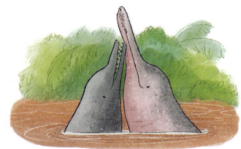

Calves are born gray but become pinkish-gray or all-pink as adults.

WHALE TYPE:
Toothed whale—river dolphin.

RANGE:
The freshwater Amazon and Orinoco rivers in South America.

"Would you like to film this whale?"

"No, he's too naughty!"

We're riding the rolling waves in the great Southern Ocean when *PING*. The ship's sonar detects something big in the water up ahead. We see a huge puff of spray from a blowhole and look over the rail. You can't believe your eyes; this magnificent gentle giant is three times the size of the research ship.

Meet the BLUE WHALE.

She navigates and communicates with other whales through a song of pulses, groans, and moans which are as loud as a jet plane and can be heard over 600 miles away.

The Antarctic blue whale is the largest animal to have ever lived on Earth. Females are larger than males and can grow to over 100 ft in length. There are five subspecies of blue whale.

Blubber is a thick layer of fat beneath a whale's skin which keeps her warm in cold seas.

She feeds by gulping huge amounts of seawater full of small shrimplike fish called krill. When she closes her mouth, she pushes the water out with her tongue through sievelike plates in the throat called baleen. The little fish are trapped in her mouth and then swallowed.

She swims alone or in pairs.

PREY:

Krill

HOW TO SPOT A BLUE WHALE:

- A huge, wide triangular tail fluke.
- A large, broad flat head.
- Baleen whales have two blowholes next to each other, a bit like nostrils.
- Mottled blue-gray back and pale underbelly.
- Streamlined body.

WHALE TYPE: Baleen whale. Instead of teeth, these whales have baleen plates, or sheets, which sieve prey from seawater.

RANGE: Found in all the oceans, blue whales migrate towards the poles during the summer months to feed and return to warmer seas in winter to have their calves.

Would you like to film this whale?

No, she's too ginormous!

Sails billow overhead and the coast is a smudge on the horizon. The yacht captain clips us onto the safety line, and we move along the rail to the front of the yacht and look down. The hull slices through the waves and a family of gray torpedo-shaped dolphins dart and leap ahead of the bow-wave, enjoying the race.

Meet the COMMON DOLPHIN.

The common dolphin is the fastest marine mammal in the world, swimming up to 37 miles per hour (mph!)

He can choose to live alone or in a pod with family or friends.

He loves to play. His favorite games are blowing bubble rings, chase, and toss the seaweed.

He enjoys swimming with other species of whales.

Sometimes lots of pods will swim together for a while to be sociable and hunt big shoals of fish.

Dolphin moms swim together in a nursery pod and help each other to raise the calves.

- **PREY:**

Octopus, Anchovy, Shrimp, Herring, Jellyfish, Salmon, Mackerel, Mullet, Squid, Crab

- **WHALE TYPE:** Toothed whale—dolphin.

- **HOW TO SPOT A COMMON DOLPHIN:**

Light to dark gray coloring.

Triangular curved-back dorsal fin.

Bands of pale gold on the sides.

A mouth shape that looks like a smile.

Would you like to film this whale?

No, he is too speedy!

- **RANGE:** Found in every ocean across the world except cold polar seas. Some pods stay in one area, while others migrate seasonally.

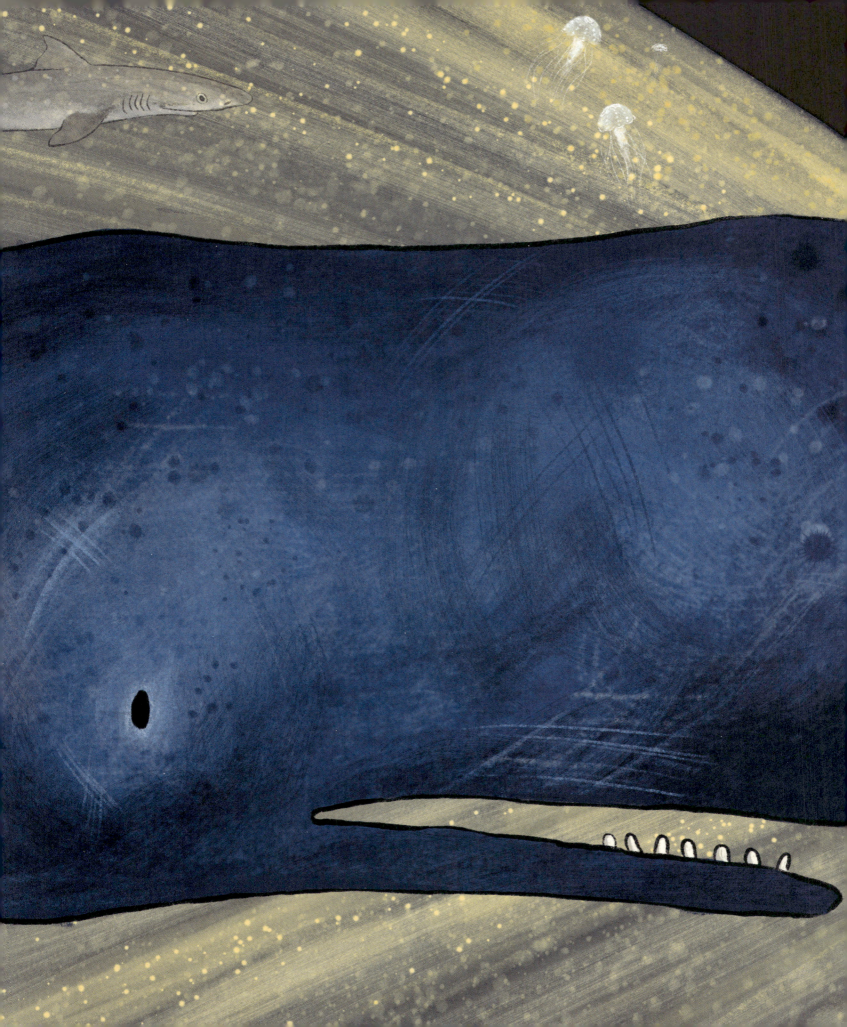

We descend into the depths of the Indian Ocean hoping to record a never-seen-before moment—a whale catching a giant squid. Toothy sharks and glowing jellyfish swim past the submarine's cameras and lights. Then, a tentacle wraps around the viewing window. Its suckers are huge! A whale charges out of the gloom and the squid jets away in a cloud of ink. Did the whale catch him? We'll never know, our submarine is too slow.

Meet the SPERM WHALE.

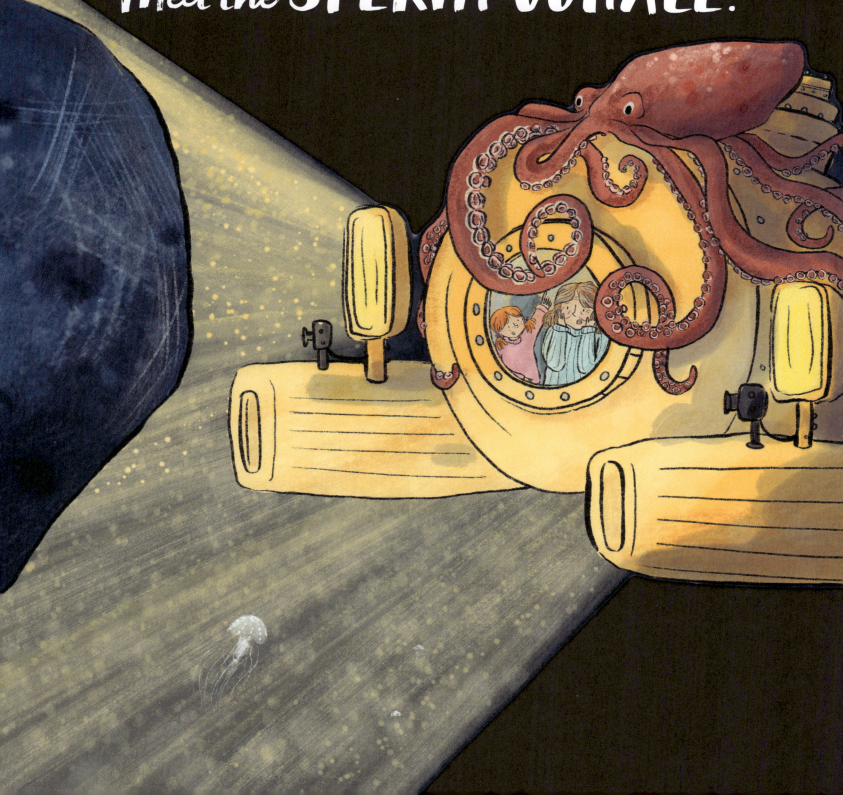

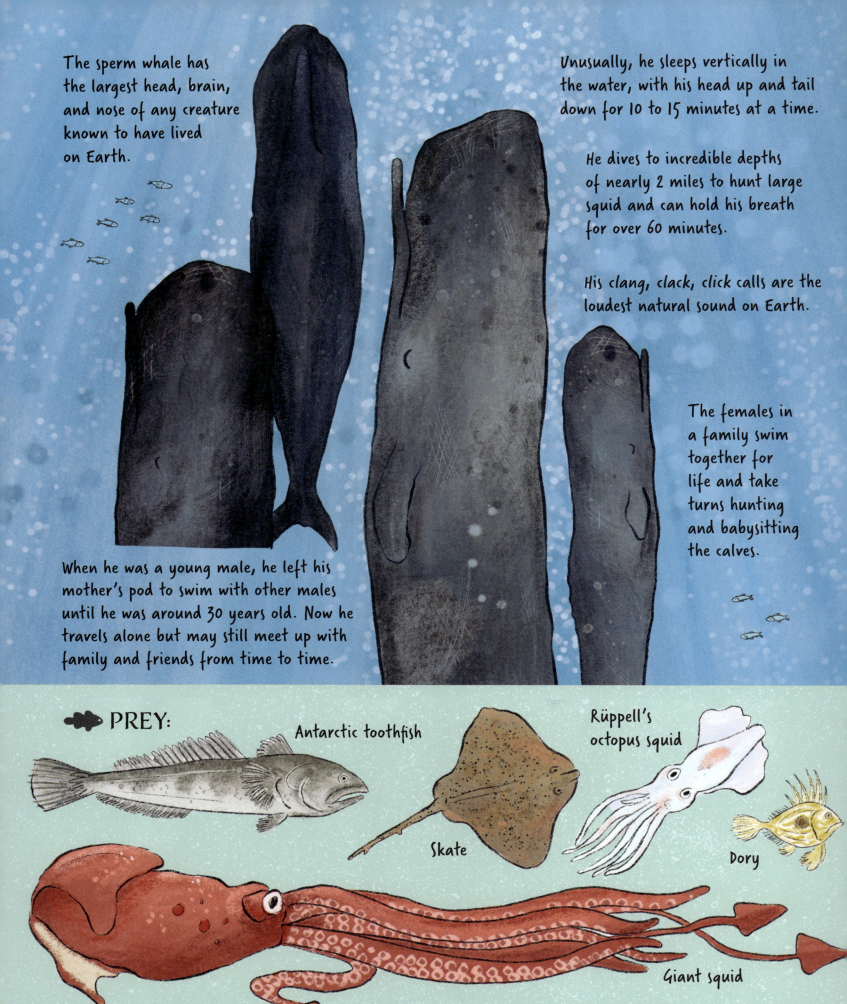

The sperm whale has the largest head, brain, and nose of any creature known to have lived on Earth.

Unusually, he sleeps vertically in the water, with his head up and tail down for 10 to 15 minutes at a time.

He dives to incredible depths of nearly 2 miles to hunt large squid and can hold his breath for over 60 minutes.

His clang, clack, click calls are the loudest natural sound on Earth.

The females in a family swim together for life and take turns hunting and babysitting the calves.

When he was a young male, he left his mother's pod to swim with other males until he was around 30 years old. Now he travels alone but may still meet up with family and friends from time to time.

PREY: Antarctic toothfish · Skate · Rüppell's octopus squid · Dory · Giant squid

We wade into the bay and snorkel along the edge of the mangrove forest, peering at the fish hiding amongst the tangle of submerged roots. Our guide waves his hand, the sign to be very still and quiet. Up ahead, a family of smooth-shaped whales dart in and out of the roots, chasing fish into the open bay where they are easier to catch.

Meet the INDO-PACIFIC FINLESS PORPOISE.

This porpoise's nickname is the Sea Pig.

She is shy of humans and boats and can quickly change direction and dart away.

Her calf sometimes rides on her back to come up for air.

She isn't as acrobatic or noisy as other whales and dolphins.

Unlike ocean dolphins, she has rectangular blunt-ended teeth to catch slippery and hard-shelled prey, such as a crab.

She uses echolocation to find prey buried in sandy sea beds or hiding behind mangrove roots.

A pod has up to 12 porpoises.

- **WHALE TYPE**: Toothed whale—porpoise.

- **HOW TO SPOT AN INDO-PACIFIC FINLESS PORPOISE:**

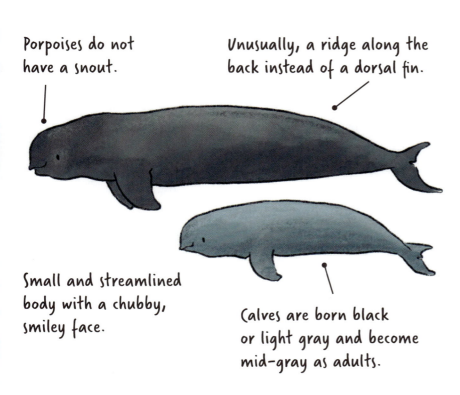

Porpoises do not have a snout.

Unusually, a ridge along the back instead of a dorsal fin.

Small and streamlined body with a chubby, smiley face.

Calves are born black or light gray and become mid-gray as adults.

- **RANGE**: Shallow coastal waters of South Asia.

"Would you like to make a film about this whale?"

"No, she's too shy!"

- **PREY:**

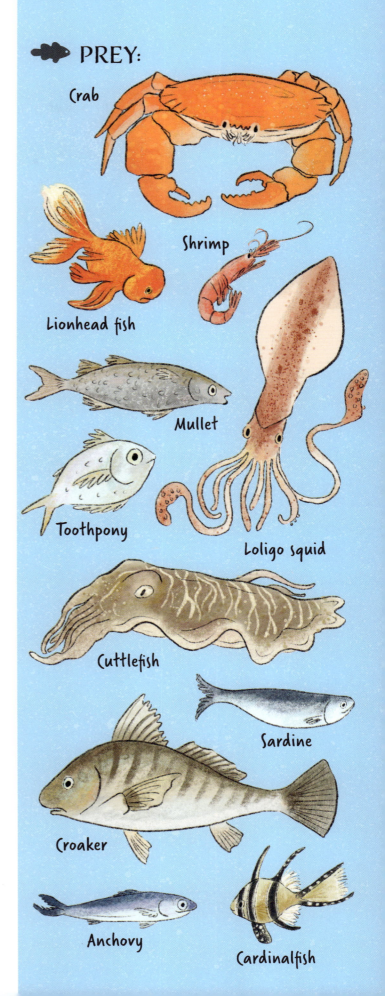

Crab

Shrimp

Lionhead fish

Mullet

Toothpony

Loligo squid

Cuttlefish

Sardine

Croaker

Anchovy

Cardinalfish

The captain drops a hydrophone over the side of the boat and we listen to some beautiful whale song. Then a whale breaches out of the water and lands on her side with a huge *SPLASH*. Her calf joins in the acrobatics, spraying water over everyone in the boat.

Meet the HUMPBACK WHALE.

Humpbacks hunt as a team. They blow rings of bubbles from their blowholes around shoals of small fish. This traps the fish close together. The whales herd the shoal upward toward the surface and then take turns gulping up hundreds of fish at a time.

She swims in a pod of up to 15 whales, but the pod doesn't stay together for long. When migrating, she travels in a smaller group.

She stays close to her calf, often touching fins, and he whisper-sings to her.

The song of a male humpback whale is a haunting tune of moans, howls, and cries. He sings while floating motionless in the water, sometimes for hours.

🐟 HOW TO SPOT A HUMPBACK WHALE:

Knobbly head and recognisable hump on the back.

Black to dark gray body and a white underbelly.

Giant mottled winglike pectoral fins—the largest in the world.

Distinctive black and white tail fluke.

🐟 WHALE TYPE: Baleen whale.

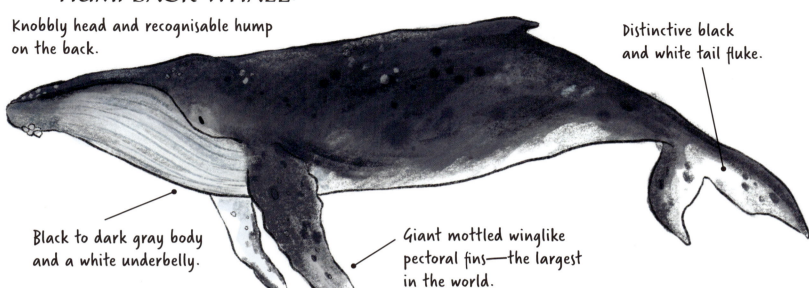

🐟 PREY:

Krill

Young herring

Capelin

🐟 RANGE: Found in all the oceans. Humpbacks have one of the longest migrations of any mammal, traveling up to 3,000 miles from polar feeding grounds in summer to tropical breeding grounds in winter.

Would you like to make a film about these whales?

Yes. They are amazing acrobats!

HERE ARE SOME OF THE HUMPBACK WHALE'S MOVES!

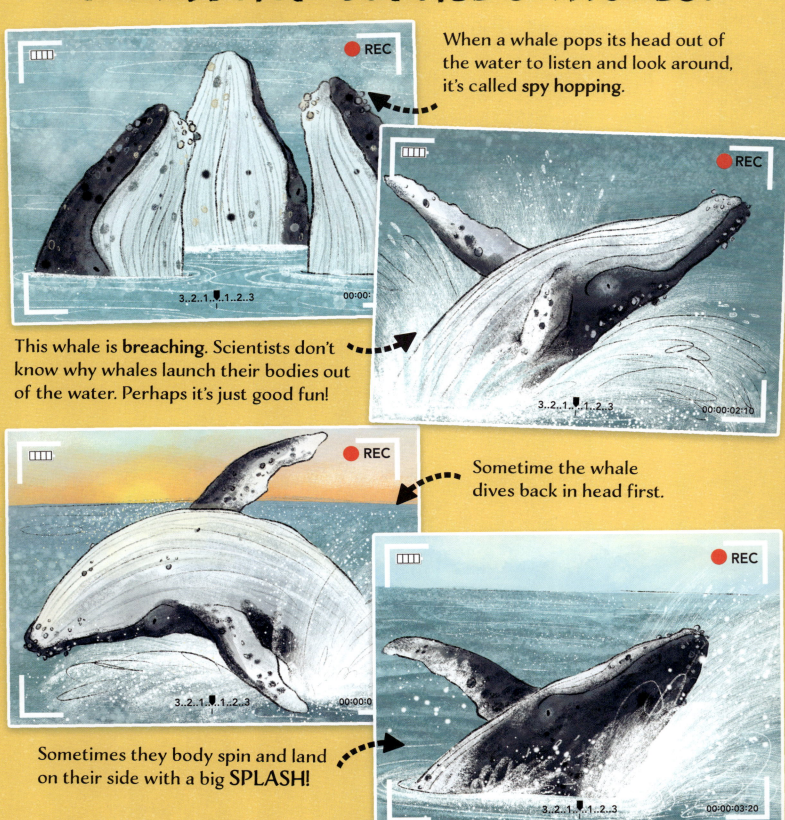

When a whale pops its head out of the water to listen and look around, it's called **spy hopping**.

This whale is **breaching**. Scientists don't know why whales launch their bodies out of the water. Perhaps it's just good fun!

Sometime the whale dives back in head first.

Sometimes they body spin and land on their side with a big **SPLASH!**

When a whale curves its back to dive down and the tail fluke rises above the surface, this is a **fluke dive**, and the perfect moment to take a photo.

Flipper slapping is when the whale rolls onto its side or back and slaps the surface with one or both pectoral fins, probably to stun and confuse fish.

This whale is **tail slapping**. It raises the back part of its body out of the water and forcefully slaps the tail fluke on the surface before diving down. Perhaps to stun and confuse fish, or to get the pod's attention and show off!

When the pod float quietly together at the surface resting, they are **logging**.

I hope you enjoyed meeting the whales!

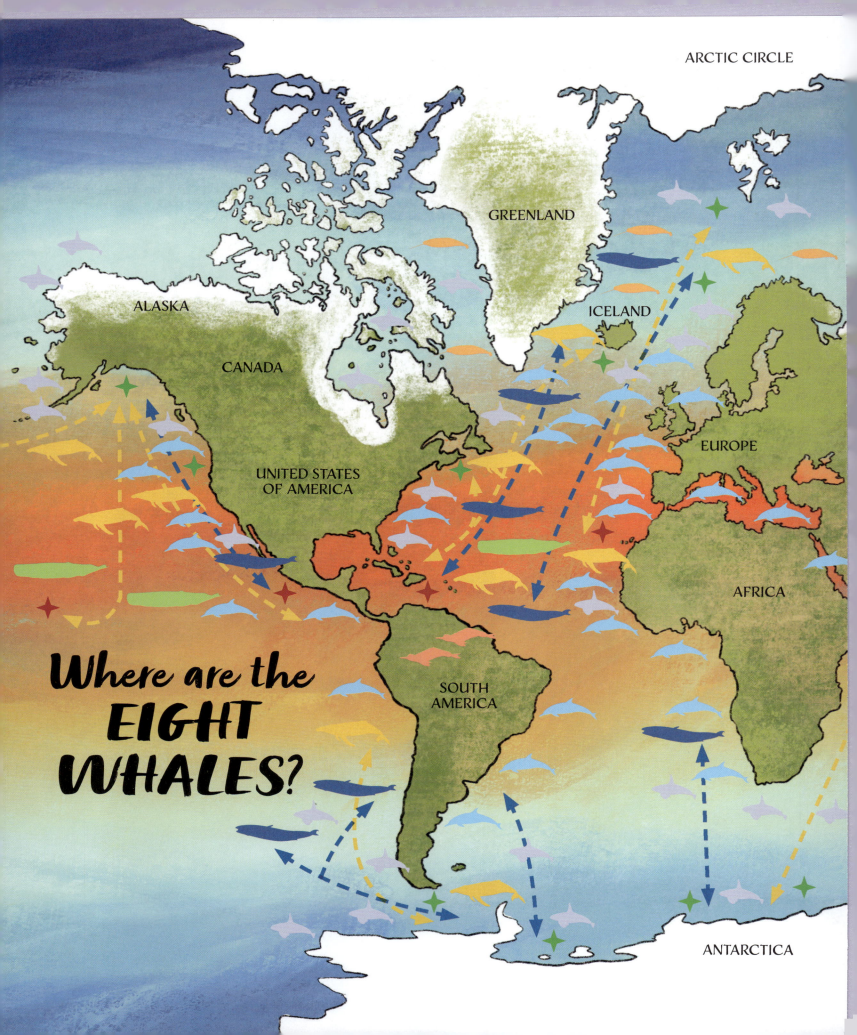

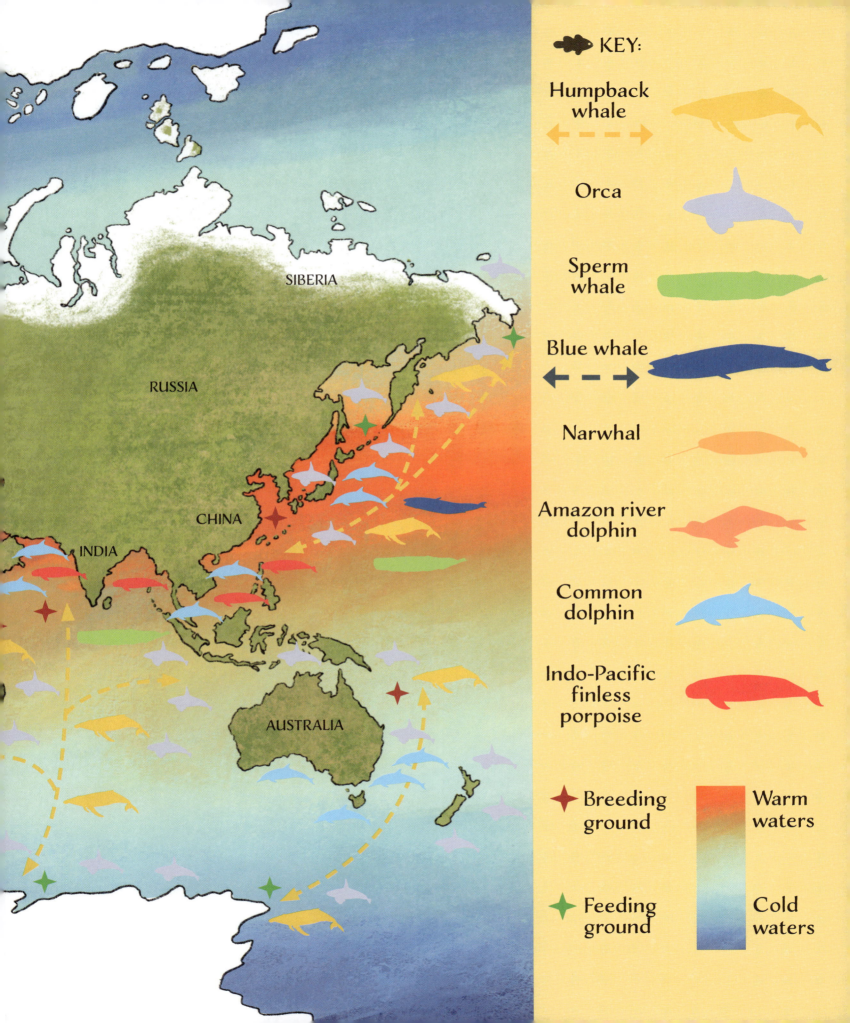

Sizing up the WHALES.

Measurement of the largest typical whale length for each species.

← 4.9 ft →
Average 6-year-old

INDO-PACIFIC FINLESS PORPOISE
Length: 6.5 ft
Weight: 155 lb

COMMON DOLPHIN
Length: 8.2 ft
Weight: 298 lb

AMAZON RIVER DOLPHIN
Length: 8.8 ft
Weight: 399 lb

NARWHAL
Length: 16.4 ft
Weight: 3,525 lb

ORCA
Length: 29.5 ft
Weight: 13,228 lb

SPERM WHALE
Length: 59 ft
Weight: 99,210 lb

HUMPBACK WHALE
Length: 59.7 ft
Weight: 80,000 lb

BLUE WHALE
Length: 109.9 ft
Weight: 418,000 lb

WHALE WATCHING TIPS

- Whales can be seen from some cliffs and beaches as well as from boats.

- Choose the right season. Whales are always on the move and may visit different places at different times of the year.

- Check the marine weather forecast and pack the right gear. Sunshine is brighter at sea and temperatures are colder.

- Keep your whale watching guidebook handy to help you identify the species of whale.

- Often, the first sign a whale is near is a puff of mist from the whale's blowhole as it surfaces to breathe out. Each species of whale has a different shape and height of blow.

- Whale watchers should always keep a respectful distance and boats should never chase a whale. Avoid making loud noises and shouting in excitement.

- Sometimes the whale may choose to swim around, alongside, or underneath the boat. This is known as **whale mugging**. Whales are not aggressive toward people. The whale is either chasing fish, being curious or playful. *Enjoy the show!*

- When a whale dives down it will rarely come up in the same spot. Note the direction it's swimming to work out where it might appear next.

- Whale watching can take many hours. Take it in turns to be **the lookout** and pack lots of snacks and games to fill the time.

- And don't forget to charge your camera battery before you go!

STRANDED WHALES
Sometimes whales become sick or confused and beach on the shore. If you see a stranded whale, don't go near the whale. Ask an adult to search the internet for the local Stranded Whale Emergency Telephone Number. With expert help, the whale could be saved and returned to the sea.

PROTECTING WHALES
In 1986, most countries in the world agreed to ban whale hunting, but whales are still at risk from human activity at sea.

Whales can be struck by boats, become tangled in fishing gear, accidentally consume plastic which makes them sick, and become confused by noisy shipping and underwater industries.

Find out how organizations in your country are protecting the whales and what you can do to help.

TO LEARN MORE ABOUT WHALES
https://iwc.int/about-whales/lives
https://happywhale.com/home
https://www.worldwildlife.org/species/whale
https://uk.whales.org/kidzone
https://www.fisheries.noaa.gov/whales
https://savethewhales.org
https://worldcetaceanalliance.org
https://whale.org